Pony Bob's Daring Ride

A PONY EXPRESS
Adventure

By Joe Bensen

Illustrated by John Potter

DISCARD

FALCON™

Helena, Mont

i

FALCON™

© 1995 by Falcon Press Publishing Co., Inc.,
Billings and Helena, Montana.

Illustrations © by John Potter.

All rights reserved, including the right to reproduce this book
or parts thereof in any form, except for inclusion of brief quotations
in a review.

Design, editing, typesetting, and other prepress work by Falcon Press,
Helena, Montana. Printed in Korea.

Library of Congress Cataloging-in-Publication Data

Bensen, Joe, 1949-
    Pony bob's daring ride : a pony express adventure / by Joe Bensen ;
illustrated by John Potter.
        p.   cm. — (Highlights from American history)
    ISBN 1-56044-263-8
    1. Pony express—History—Juvenile literature. 2. Postal service—
United States—History—Juvenile literature. 3. West (U.S.)—
History—1860-1890—Juvenile literature. I. Potter, John, 1957-
. II. Title. III. Series.
    HE6375.P65B46   1994
    383'.143'097809034—dc20   94-46348
                                                         CIP
                                                         AC

Contents

The Mail Must Go Through

Bob Haslam was exhausted—and it wasn't only because he'd ridden fifty miles that day. The Pony Express rider also was anxious about news that an Indian war was brewing.

Only a couple of hours earlier, when Haslam had stopped to change horses in Carson City, Nevada, he'd learned that the Paiutes had recently killed five men at Williams Station. When he reached Miller's Station, he discovered that all the horses there had been taken for use in the coming conflict. There was nothing he could do but coax another fifteen miles out of his tired mare.

Haslam decided to continue east to Buckland's Station, where he would pass the mail to the next rider. As he rode along the Carson River, not far from Williams Station, he kept a sharp eye on the wooded hills around him.

Now, as he approached Buckland's, something seemed wrong. Where was the rider who was supposed to relieve him? The man should have been standing in front of the station with his horse saddled, ready to take the mail pouch and continue eastward. Instead, Haslam was met by the station keeper, a fellow named Marley.

The two entered the small station, where Haslam found Johnson Richardson, the next rider, sulking in a corner. When Haslam asked him why he wasn't ready to ride, Richardson argued that it was suicide to travel the trail now that war with the Indians was certain. He thought it made more sense to wait a few days for word from Bolivar Roberts, the district supervisor for this section of the Pony Express.

Haslam could tell that Richardson felt uneasy about refusing to ride. The man wouldn't even look Haslam in the eye. But Haslam also knew it was pointless to argue. In fact, he couldn't blame Richardson for being cautious.

Still, when Marley asked Haslam if he would take over Richardson's section—more than one hundred miles east to Smith Creek—Haslam didn't hesitate to say yes. Maybe it was his sense of duty. He knew that he was the only one who could get the mail through on schedule. But more likely it was because Haslam was only nineteen years old and the idea of an adventure thrilled him.

Marley was relieved that Haslam had agreed to ride on. He knew that the young man had been hand-picked by the district supervisor for his toughness and expert riding ability.

Outside, the stock tender had already transferred the mail pouches to a fresh horse. He knew Haslam liked his horses half-wild and full of fire, and this one certainly fit that description.

Haslam leaped into the saddle, and the mustang reared back on its hind legs. The young man smiled at the surge of power beneath him. Then he headed up the trail at a lope, turning in his saddle to wave farewell to the men at Buckland's Station.

A Great American Adventure

Haslam knew when he took the job that he might have days like this. In fact, part of the attraction of becoming an express rider was the danger and excitement.

The Pony Express had started delivering mail just six weeks earlier, in the first week of April 1860. It offered an important and speedy new way for people on opposite sides of the continent to communicate with each other.

Before 1860, the settled part of the United States ended at about the Missouri-Kansas border. Both railroad and telegraph lines went no farther west than St. Joseph, a town on the Missouri River. Beyond was a huge wilderness—nearly two thousand miles of prairie, mountain, and desert stretching all the way to the new state of California. Only a small number of settlements existed—except for the Mormon communities in Utah and a few isolated forts.

There was also little if any mail service. This was a matter of concern for the people of California. Since 1848, when the rush to the California gold fields had begun, the population of the new state had grown quickly. Nearly all of the pioneers had just moved there from the East and Midwest, and there was a great demand for news from back home.

But mail between California and the rest of the United States had to go either by ship by way of Panama, or by stagecoach through Texas and Arizona. Either way, it could take a month for the mail to get through—if it got through at all. The folks in California felt cut off from the rest of the country.

In 1860, the stagecoach company of Russell, Majors, and Waddell announced plans for a faster and more direct mail service between St. Joseph, Missouri, and Sacramento, California. Teams of riders would carry mail back and forth between the two cities by relay. By changing horses and riders regularly, the Pony Express hoped to transport mail almost two thousand miles in just ten days.

Each rider would carry the mail in a *mochila*, a flat piece of leather with four small boxes attached to the corners. The mochila was designed to fit over a light saddle. When a rider changed horses, he just pulled the mochila from the saddle and threw it onto the saddle of a fresh horse. This allowed him to change mounts and perhaps grab a quick drink of water in less than two minutes.

The organizers of the Pony Express already had established many stations along the route their stagecoaches traveled. Between these stations they added smaller ones, where their express riders could change horses. At first, these small stations were placed about twenty-five miles apart, but the distance was later reduced to about ten miles. This meant that the riders could push their horses hard and change them often. At each of these stations was a station keeper, a stock tender, and at least two fresh horses.

About every one hundred miles along the route was a home station, where each rider would pass the mail to the next carrier. The weary rider then stayed at the station until the man bringing mail from the opposite direction arrived. Then he transported this mail back to his original starting point. This meant that each rider traveled only a small section of the trail, carrying mail in both directions.

The founders of the Pony Express didn't expect it to make money. They merely wanted to prove that their route across the middle of the country was the best way to travel between East and West. If they could do this, they might be able to attract profitable government mail contracts.

And so, just five weeks before an Indian uprising, this ex-

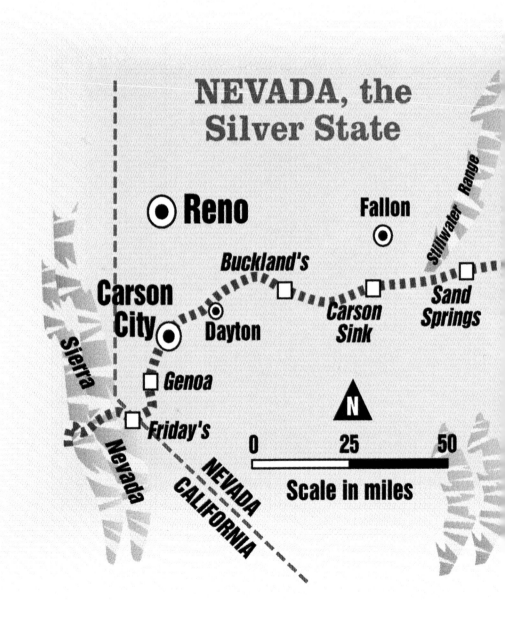

periment in speedy communication began. It would prove to be a glorious chapter in the history of the American frontier.

It would also be a rough and dangerous undertaking for the young riders and the brave men who manned the remote stations. And the roughest, most dangerous stretch of all ran straight across Nevada.

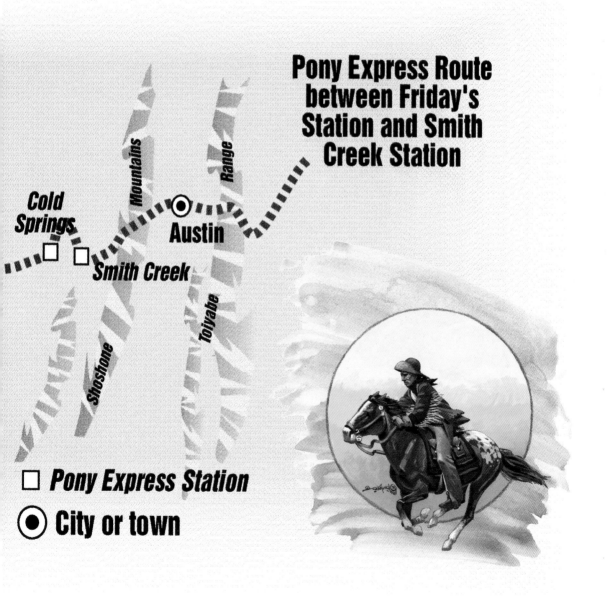

Pony Express Route between Friday's Station and Smith Creek Station

Cold Springs

Mountains

Range

Austin

Smith Creek

Shoshone

Toiyabe

☐ **Pony Express Station**

◉ **City or town**

The Young Riders

—WANTED—

Young, skinny, wiry fellows not over eighteen.

Must be expert riders, willing to risk death daily.

Orphans preferred. Wages $25 per week.

Apply, PONY EXPRESS STABLES

St. Joseph, Missouri

—early advertisement for riders

The Pony Express needed special men to deliver the mail. They would have to ride long hours in all weather across rough and dangerous territory. It was clear from the start that not just anyone would do.

Most of the men who were hired *were* over eighteen, but usually not by much. They had to be tough, brave, and hard-working. They also were screened for what the owners called "high moral quality." They had to pledge not to drink alcohol, use profanity, or get into fights. But above all, they had to be first-rate horsemen. Young men competed for the prized positions in riding contests held outside the Pony Express offices.

Those who were hired were expected

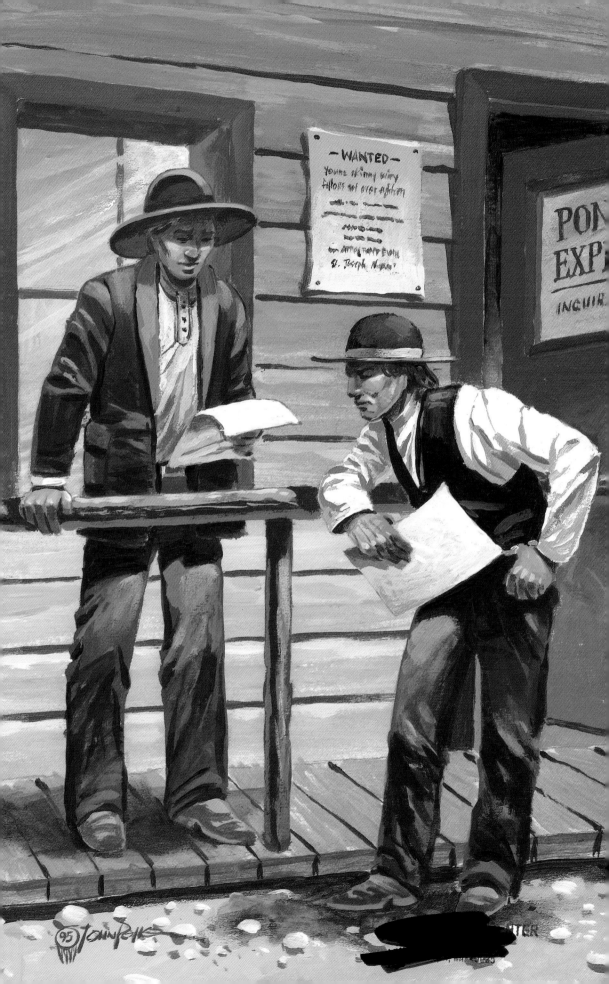

to ride as much as four hundred miles every week, making two trips in each direction. Considering the rough conditions and the constant pressure of having to stick to the schedule no matter what, it's no wonder so many riders dropped out. Though there were never more than eighty riders employed at any one time, as many as two hundred young men are known to have ridden for "the Pony."

Still, in spite of the strict selection process and the difficulties of the job, the Pony Express never lacked riders. The pay was good—at least fifty dollars a month, plus room and board. That may not sound like much today, but at the time it was generous—more than three times the pay of a cavalry soldier.

It was considered a great honor to work for the Pony Express. Riders were admired and respected wherever they went. But perhaps more attractive than the pay and the prestige was the opportunity for adventure. For a young man of the 1860s, it was like being an astronaut or a professional athlete.

Just as important as the quality of the riders was the quality of the horses that carried them. The Pony Express bought five hundred of the very best animals available, paying up to four times the cost of average horses. For the prairie country on the eastern end of the route, it used the fastest thorough-bred stock it could find. For the rough desert and mountain country west of Fort Laramie, it used native mustangs prized for their toughness and endurance.

Though all the horses worked hard on the trail, they received excellent care. They dined on a rich diet of grains designed to keep them stronger and faster than grass-fed Indian ponies. Their young riders depended on them not only for safe delivery of the mail, but for their very lives.

The Paiute War

Bob Haslam knew all about the Paiute Indians. Like most of his fellow riders, he'd grown up in Indian country and learned early in life to respect the ways of the Native Americans.

The Paiutes lived in the rugged mountains and desert of what is now the state of Nevada. Though the country was rough and inhospitable, it was *their* country, and they resented the growing number of white settlers who were intruding upon their hunting grounds.

The Indians believed that the land belonged to no one. The Earth was to be shared by all people. But how do you share with people who won't share with you, who put up fences to keep you away from all the best land and water? This was what the Paiutes wondered about the white newcomers.

At first, there was little friction between the two peoples. Most of this land was so forbidding that the whites had no interest in staying. They only wanted to cross the desert to reach the rich mining districts of the Sierra Nevada and the fertile valleys of California.

But soon whites realized that they could establish farms and ranches in the well-watered valley of the Carson River. Silver strikes in the hills above the valley began to draw more and more fortune hunters. The Paiutes began to worry about the growing number of intruders.

The winter of 1859-1860 was especially difficult for the Paiutes. Many women and children died of hunger and cold. Some of the younger braves blamed the trouble on evil spirits brought by the White Man. Finally, in May 1860, the Paiutes went on the warpath in a desperate attempt to keep control of their homeland. Two-thirds of the Nevada stretch of the Pony Express route now ran through hostile territory.

Alone in the Desert

Bob Haslam had left his home station near the south end of Lake Tahoe on May 9, amid growing fear and hostility. He'd changed horses at the Mormon settlement of Genoa and again at Carson City, where he'd gotten a hint of the trouble that was brewing.

Now, Haslam left Buckland's and headed east across twenty-seven miles of rugged desert to Carson Sink Station. Nervous as he was, he urged his high-spirited horse to stretch out its stride and make the dust fly.

Carson Sink got its name from the way nearby Carson Lake disappears, or "sinks," into the desert. Because there were no trees or rocks there, the Pony Express station had been made of adobe, a sort of hardened mud.

The station keeper and stock tender must have been surprised to see Haslam rather than Richardson approaching. And it couldn't have made them very comfortable to learn of the Indian war. Haslam was glad to get a fresh horse under him. He traded mounts again at Sand Springs and Cold Springs stations. As he sped across the barren desert, he had to sympathize with Richardson. This was the most desolate and dangerous part of the entire Pony Express route. He stayed constantly on the lookout for hostile Indians.

From Cold Springs, the trail climbed into the mountains. The narrow canyon was a perfect spot for an ambush. But the

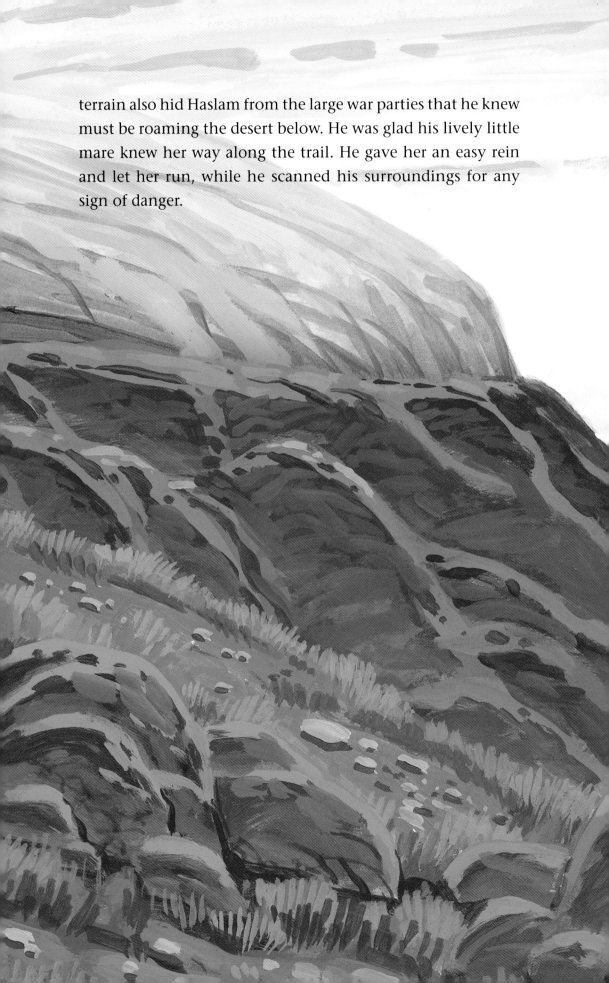

terrain also hid Haslam from the large war parties that he knew must be roaming the desert below. He was glad his lively little mare knew her way along the trail. He gave her an easy rein and let her run, while he scanned his surroundings for any sign of danger.

It was dark as he neared Smith Creek Station, and he realized he had ridden more than 160 miles since morning. He was so tired that his body felt numb. He was thankful that he could finally turn the mochila over to a new rider, Jay Kelley. Haslam told Kelley and the station hands about the Indian war to the west. Then Kelley galloped off into the darkness. He would speed both the mail and news of the Paiute uprising to the stations farther east.

Haslam could hardly walk. The station keeper helped him into the cabin and fixed him a quick supper. Then Haslam fell into the most welcome sleep of his life. He'd been in the saddle, riding hard, for more than eighteen hours.

Back in the Saddle

Had he really slept six hours already? It seemed like his head had just hit the rolled-up jacket he was using as a pillow. But now the station keeper was shaking him gently, rousing him from a deep sleep.

The westbound rider had come in, exhausted, with the next pouch of mail from the East. Haslam would have to carry it on without delay. He rose in the darkness and pulled on his boots. After splashing his face with cold water, he stuffed some biscuits and dried meat into his jacket pocket. Outside, the stock tender held the reins of a freshly saddled horse.

Haslam raced out of the mountains, covering the twenty-three miles back to Cold Springs in less than two hours. Time was always a factor on these rides, but today it was more than just a matter of staying on schedule. This was no safe place to poke along.

As he approached Cold Springs Station, his heart sank. From half a mile away, he could see a faint wisp of smoke curling above the horizon, and he doubted it was from a cooking fire. As he rode closer, he saw that the place was a wreck and there were no horses in the corral.

His hand went automatically to the handle of his Colt revolver, and he peered nervously around him. Everything was still—horribly still. When he reached the smoking ruins of the station, he saw the keeper's body, riddled with arrows, lying in

the doorway. Haslam shuddered. His first thought was to put the spurs to his horse and get out of there, but he had the good sense to stop to feed and water the animal first.

It was thirty-four miles to Sand Springs Station. He had no doubt that his horse could get him there, but would it be able to outrun a Paiute war party after such a hard ride? And what would he find at Sand Springs?

Haslam had to resist the temptation to speed across the desert. It would be a disaster to wear out his horse and then run into Indian warriors. He was glad it was a lively and healthy animal.

After three nerve-racking hours, Haslam reached Sand Springs. He was relieved to find the station undamaged and two fresh horses in the corral. He was met by a lone stock tender, who by this time had heard more than he wanted about the hostility raging throughout the region. The station keeper had left that morning for Carson Sink Station, where he hoped to find an extra man to bring back to reinforce Sand Springs. Haslam had no trouble convincing the stock tender to abandon his post and ride with him to Carson Sink. A description of the smoking ruins at Cold Springs was all it took to get the stock tender to saddle the second horse.

Out of the Wilderness

Inside the adobe station at Carson Sink, they found fifteen men who had gathered from the surrounding region for protection. The men were terrified, because they had just seen a scouting party of about fifty Paiutes.

Haslam left the stock tender at Carson Sink and rode on alone to Buckland's. He knew that the closer he came to the settlements in the Carson Valley, the safer he would be. But he was still in dangerous territory, and the news of the Paiute scouts had spooked him. He pushed his horse as hard as he could.

By the time he reached Buckland's, Haslam was exhausted once again. Marley, the station keeper, was overjoyed to see that the young rider was safe and that he had gotten the mail through in both directions. He made Haslam rest for a couple of hours before starting the last fifty-five miles to his home station at Lake Tahoe. He thought Haslam would be safer if he rode at night, and the young man was too tired to argue.

On a fresh horse, in the cool night air, Haslam headed down into the Carson Valley. At Carson City, he visited for a few minutes with his boss, Bolivar Roberts. As Haslam described the tense situation to the east, many anxious men listened in on the conversation. The people of Carson City were eager for any news of Indian movement.

West of Carson, Haslam could feel safer from Indian attack. Now, it was just a matter of fighting the exhaustion that crept over him. Several times during the long climb out of the valley into the Sierra Nevada, he nodded off, falling asleep right in the saddle. Once again, he was glad that his horse knew its way along the trail.

In the middle of the night, half asleep and numb with cold and hunger, Haslam finished his ride where he had started two days earlier. He had ridden more than three hundred miles through dangerous country in the midst of a major Indian war. He had made what would turn out to be the longest and most daring ride in the history of the Pony Express. For the rest of his life, he would be known as "Pony Bob."

A Short and Terrible War

As Haslam was making his historic ride across Nevada, the most dramatic events of the Paiute War were unfolding.

After the attack on Williams Station, the residents of Carson City were stirred to action. A group of about one hundred well-armed volunteers rode out to teach the Indians a lesson at about the same time that Haslam was starting back from Smith Creek.

They rode north out of the Carson Valley, full of brash talk and high spirits. They had little respect for the fighting skills of the Paiutes. In fact, they were as over-confident as Lieutenant Colonel George Custer would be sixteen years later, when he and his men attacked a Sioux and Cheyenne encampment on the Little Bighorn River.

The Paiutes lured the militia into a clever trap and killed almost half of them in a fierce battle. The rest of the volunteers retreated hastily to Carson City.

In the next three weeks, seven Pony Express stations were destroyed, sixteen employees killed, and 150 horses stolen. Just after Haslam headed west from Smith Creek, the station there was attacked. The day after he convinced the stock tender at Sand Springs to abandon that station, it was destroyed by a war party.

The solitary Pony Express riders and their isolated stations were more vulnerable to attack than wagon trains or towns. At Dry Creek Station, a little east of Smith Creek, a badly wounded rider fell from his saddle and died—but the mail he had carried went on.

The grim conditions that spring prompted several riders to quit the company. At the end of May, the Pony Express suspended service for three weeks. This caused a huge outcry among the settlements west of Nevada. The people of California had fought hard to get fast mail service, and they weren't happy about being cut off once again.

Partly because of the closing of the Pony Express, California sent troops and supplies to help the Nevada settlers end the Indian uprising. The Paiutes were forced north out of the Carson Valley. After a couple of small battles, they disappeared into the desert and mountains they knew so well.

To help protect the settlers of Nevada from further Indian raids, the U.S. Army built Fort Churchill just a few miles from Buckland's Station.

By the middle of June, the war was over. The Pony Express rebuilt its ruined stations and resumed service. It delivered the mail continuously for the next sixteen months.

The End of the Trail

In late October 1861, telegraph lines from the East and West finally were joined in Salt Lake City, bringing to an end the need for the Pony Express. The unique mail service had lasted only nineteen months. Its owners had lost hundreds of thousands of dollars, and the valuable mail contracts they had counted on were awarded to a competing stage company. In business terms, the Pony Express was a disaster.

But in other ways, it was not a failure. It proved once and for all that the overland route across the middle of the country was practical. A few years later, workers would lay the tracks of the first transcontinental railroad over the very trails traveled by Pony Bob and his fellow riders.

But the most important contribution of the Pony Express was that it linked California and the western territories to the Union at the start of the Civil War. Maybe the outcome of the war between the states would have been different if California and the rich mining districts of Nevada had sided with the South.

Because of their fame and youth, former Pony Express riders were in great demand for many exciting jobs. The Civil War and the settlement of the American West provided opportunities for many of them to remain in the saddle as soldiers or army scouts. Several became wealthy from mining and other business ventures. Four Utah riders went on to become Mormon bishops.

The most famous Pony rider of all was a fellow named William Cody, who went on to be a scout, hunter, and showman—the legendary Buffalo Bill.

Many riders and station keepers found work with the new stagecoach lines and express mail companies that were starting up throughout the West. Bob Haslam went to work for the Wells Fargo Company in Idaho and Montana. When he tired of riding the trails, he served as Deputy U.S. Marshal in Salt Lake City. Eventually, he moved to Chicago, where he lived peacefully until the age of seventy-two.

Today, the image of the solitary Pony Express rider—like the lonely prospector, the cowboy, the Indian warrior, and the cavalry soldier—is one of the great symbols of the Wild West.